Let's Draw!

Action!

Leon Baxter

Collins
in association with
🐚 Belitha Press

Let's draw together . . .

In the first six *Let's Draw!* books you discovered the basic principles of line, colour, movement, shape and proportion. If you have tried all those ideas, you should now be feeling more confident about making pictures.

In these new books I am encouraging you to be observant and inventive so that you will enjoy your drawing even more. You can learn how to compose and construct your pictures, how to create space and movement, and even how to have three-dimensional fun with paper itself.

Don't use a ruler. Draw all straight lines freehand. This is a good exercise for getting your eyes and hands to work together. Try out some of these ideas. Use your imagination and see your paper come to life.

Things you will need:

coloured pencils	paint	glue
crayons	sticky coloured paper	brushes
pastels	lots of drawing paper	scissors
felt-tip pens	(white and coloured)	

Have a good time!

Leon Baxter

First published 1989 by William Collins Sons and Co Ltd
in association with Belitha Press Limited,
31 Newington Green, London N16 9PU
Text and illustrations in this format copyright © Belitha Press 1989
Text and illustrations copyright © Leon Baxter 1989
Art Director: Treld Bicknell   Editor: Carol Watson
ISBN 0 00 197796 2
Typesetting by Chambers Wallace, London
Printed in Italy

Action!

Here is a picture sequence.
It tells an action story.

The action is shown by bending and stretching lines and by
drawing something about to happen or that has happened.
This gives the suggestion of time.

Let's begin by looking at how we move.

How do we walk?

To keep your balance you swing your arms in the opposite direction to your legs. Like this:

He's right.

Can you draw a boy walking?

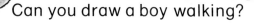

To run, I bend my back and legs.

Now draw him running.

4

The race

This boy is doing exercises.

bending

stretching

running
on the
spot

Can you draw a girl doing the same exercises?

Now draw the other athletes in the race.

How to suggest time

In these three pictures we can show:

before	during	after

1. He is going to kick the ball.

2. He is kicking the ball.

3. He has kicked the ball.

Now draw someone kicking the ball.

1. before

2. during

3. after

before	during	after
1. She is going to throw the ball.	2. She is throwing the ball.	3. She has thrown the ball.

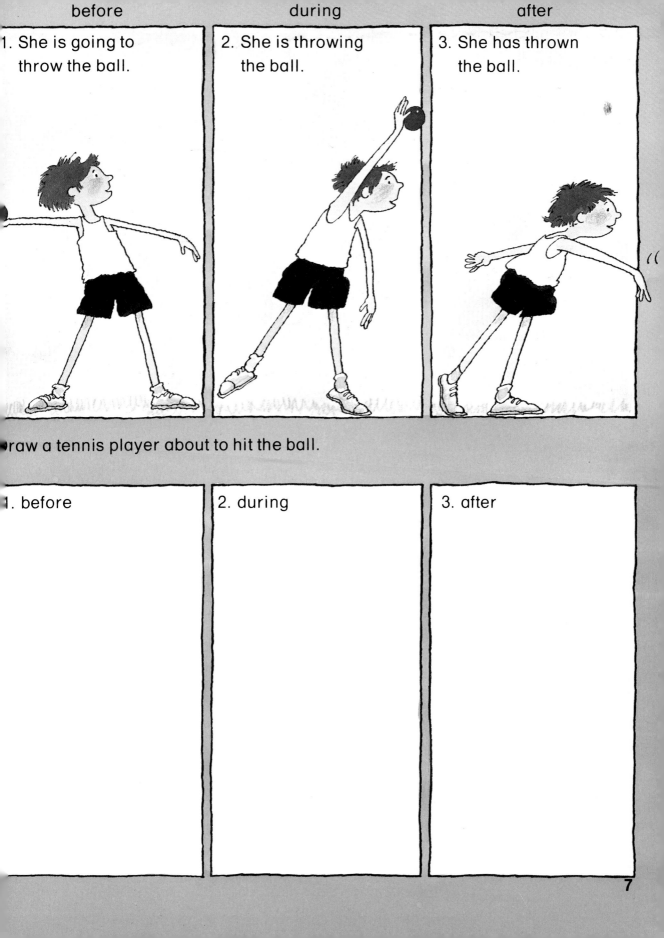

Draw a tennis player about to hit the ball.

1. before	2. during	3. after

Action sequences

Here are two sequences showing people enjoying a holiday.
One sequence of actions takes place in a very short space
of time while the other takes place over a much longer
period. Some actions are all over in seconds, others fill
days or weeks. By changing the backgrounds, showing
travel and a change of climate, you can suggest the
passage of time.

Choose summer or winter and make a holiday picture.
Draw all the things you like to do.

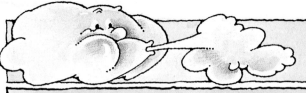

Make the wind blow

The wind is blowing
this way: ←

Draw a flag flying
this way: →

Draw a tree with the
wind blowing this way: ←

Draw a line of washing dancing in the wind.
The wind is blowing this way: →

This boy is going for a walk.

Drawing a strong breeze will help him on his way.

Draw a storm with the boy hurrying home.

These planes are giving an aerobatic display.

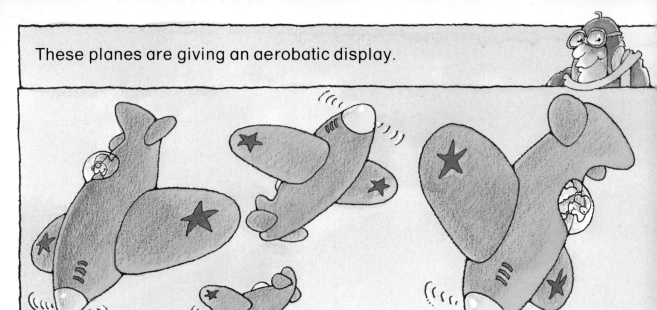

Draw your own planes – make them dive, climb and roll.

Helicopters put their tails up when they take off.

Draw a helicopter taking off.

Sailing boats lean over as they zip along.

Draw a boat sailing in a strong wind.

Motor bikes can jump.

Draw a motor bike jumping a ditch.

Moviemaking

These men are filming a stuntman driving a car over a cliff.

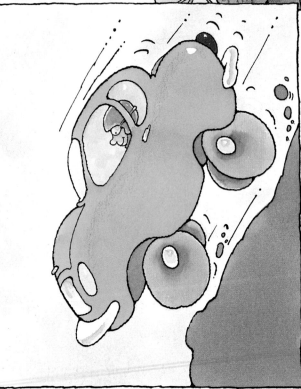

Draw your favourite action scene in these four frames.

These quarry men are using high explosives to blast rock from a cliff face.

16

Finish this picture. Show the volcano blowing its top!

Fun at the fair

There is lots of action at the fair.
Finish this big picture.

Mini-movies

You can make your own movies, by using a paper cylinder that spins on the turntable of a record player set at 45 rpm. The movie is drawn on a paper strip placed inside the cylinder.
You watch through slits cut in the cylinder.

To make a 12-frame cartoon movie you will need:

1. A strip of stiff paper or card 500 mm × 150 mm which is black on one side and white on the other.

2. A strip of cartridge paper 480 mm × 70 mm for the movie strip.

3. A pencil, ruler, pair of scissors, black felt-tip pen, paper paste, 2 paper clips and a record player.

The cylinder is made from a strip of stiff paper or card. If you cannot buy black and white paper or card, colour one side of the strip with a black felt-tip pen. Paint, crayons or pastels are too messy. There are twelve slits – draw them onto the strip and carefully cut them out. All measurements are shown below.

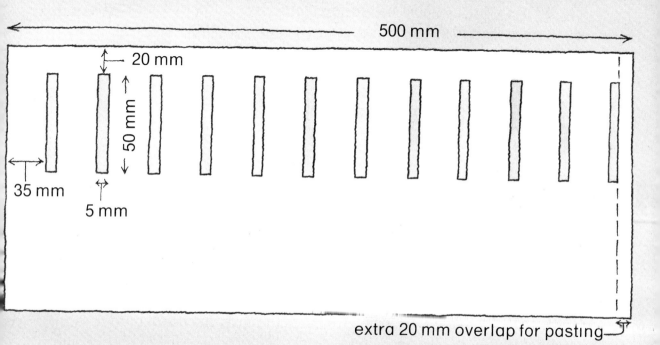

500 mm

20 mm

50 mm

35 mm

5 mm

extra 20 mm overlap for pasting

Now paste the two ends of the strip together with a 20 mm overlap. The **black** surface should be on the outside.

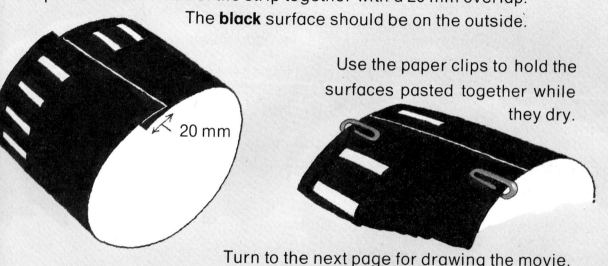

20 mm

Use the paper clips to hold the surfaces pasted together while they dry.

Turn to the next page for drawing the movie.

Drawing the movie

Draw or trace the 12 pictures on the opposite page onto the strip of cartridge paper (480 mm × 70 mm). Use a black felt-tip pen to colour the man in.

Showing the movie

Keeping the picture on the *inside*, bring the two ends of the movie strip together and place it inside the cylinder, like this:

Put the cylinder onto the turntable of your record player — making sure it is central. Now switch on. Look through the slits and watch your man doing headstands!
Use the same cylinder to make your own movies.

Note that the action runs backwards from right to left.

A paper strip 480 mm × 70 mm divides into 12 frames, each 40 mm wide. Draw your picture in each frame like this.

Keep it simple — experiment with colour and all kinds of action.

1

2

3

4

5

6

7

8

9

10

11

12

What happened?

Here are the beginning and end of the story.
Can you draw what happened in between?